HAPPY Birthday Grandfather

The Life Graduate Publishing Group

No part of this book may be scanned, reproduced or distributed in any printed or electronic form without the prior permission of the author or publisher.

Copyright - The Life Graduate Publishing Group 2020 - All Rights Reserved

We love to receive reviews from our customers. If you had the opportunity to provide a review we would greatly appreciate it.
Thank you!

Birthday
I Wrote This Book For You Grandfather!

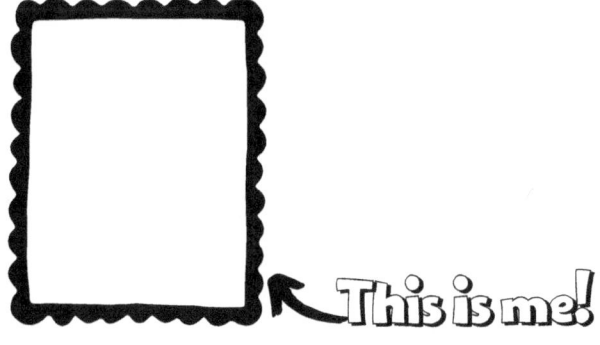
← This is me!

Created By: _____
Birthday Year: _____
My Age: _____ yrs

We celebrate your birthday on..

MONTH _____

DAY _____

I love birthday cake!!

Happy Birthday Grandfather. I wrote this book for you because......

_____

_____

_____

_____

This is a drawing of us together on your birthday.

Grandfather and I

4

I LOVE YOU BECAUSE...

_____

_____

_____

_____

5

Grandfather, my favorite place to visit with you is....

These are 3 things you do that are kind.

_____

_____

_____

My favorite birthday food is...

Place your hand here and trace around it with a pencil

You like to relax by doing this..

_____

_____

_____

_____

My favorite photo!

I would like you to teach me how to do this...

If I could get you anything in the whole wide-world for your birthday it would be...

You make me laugh when..

If I created a birthday t-shirt for you, it would look like this...

Create your special design here!

It might look like this or something different?

You can do this better than anyone else!

This is a drawing of us on your birthday.

I hope that one day we can do this together..

You cook the best......

I colored in this birthday cake for you!

Remember to draw on the candles!

These are 3 words that best describe you.

1. _____

2. _____

3. _____

SPECIAL MOMENTS or MEMORIES

Add other special photo's or drawings here ↙

SPECIAL MOMENTS or MEMORIES

Add other special photo's or drawings here

SPECIAL MOMENTS or MEMORIES

Add other special photo's or drawings here ↙

SPECIAL MOMENTS or MEMORIES

Add other special photo's or drawings here ↙

Color me in!

THIS HAS BEEN MY SPECIAL BIRTHDAY GIFT THAT I HAVE CREATED FOR YOU.

I HOPE YOU LIKE IT!

A sample of other books created by Romney Nelson

www.thelifegraduate.com/bookstore

www.ingramcontent.com/pod-product-compliance
Lightning Source LLC
LaVergne TN
LVHW060144080526
838202LV00049B/4081